LET'S GET A PET!

MY FIRST BUNNY

By Joan Stoltman

Gareth Stevens PUBLISHING

Please visit our website, www.garethstevens.com. For a free color catalog of all our high-quality books, call toll free 1-800-542-2595 or fax 1-877-542-2596.

Cataloging-in-Publication Data

Names: Stoltman, Joan.
Title: My first bunny / Joan Stoltman.
Description: New York : Gareth Stevens Publishing, 2018. | Series: Let's get a pet! | Includes index.
Identifiers: ISBN 9781482464412 (pbk.) | ISBN 9781482464436 (library bound) | ISBN 9781482464429 (6 pack)
Subjects: LCSH: Rabbits–Juvenile literature. | Rabbits as pets.
Classification: LCC SF453.2 S76 2018 | DDC 636.9'322–dc23

Published in 2018 by
Gareth Stevens Publishing
111 East 14th Street, Suite 349
New York, NY 10003

Designer: Bethany Perl
Editor: Joan Stoltman

Photo credits: p. 1 AlohaHawaii/Shutterstock.com; pp. 2–24 (background texture) Liliya Mulyukova/Shutterstock.com; p. 5 Aprilphoto/Shutterstock.com; p. 7 Natasha Sioss/Moment Open/Getty Images; p. 9 rodho/Shutterstock.com; p. 11 Bronwyn Photo/Shutterstock.com; p. 13 TippaPatt/Shutterstock/com; p. 15 anetapics/Shutterstock.com; p. 17 Daniel Rajszczak/Shutterstock.com; p. 19 Nadezda Murmakova/Shutterstock.com; p. 21 (castor rex, lop-eared rex) Rosa Jay/Shutterstock.com; p. 21 (Dutch) IrinaK/Shutterstock.com; p. 21 (French lop) Stieber/Shutterstock.com.

Printed in the United States of America

CPSIA compliance information: Batch #CS17GS: For further information contact Gareth Stevens, New York, New York at 1-800-542-2595.

CONTENTS

Boldface words appear in the glossary.

It's Bunny Time!

Can you think of anything cuter than a fuzzy bunny? Bunnies make great pets! They're quiet and fun to watch. Once they feel safe in your home, they can be silly, playful, and sometimes even **affectionate**!

Making Bunny Feel at Home

Bunnies are most **comfortable** on the floor. Put your new bunny's **hutch** or pen in a family or common room. Then put in some cardboard tubes and boxes, ropes, and old towels. Those are all great bunny chew toys!

Bunnies should have at least 2 hours out of their hutch each day. Be sure to "bunny proof" first! This includes putting away books, cords, papers, and toys. Bunnies love to chew on everything!

Clean Bunny

It's easy to keep bunnies clean because they **groom** themselves! You can help by softly brushing them a few times a week. They're also easy to keep clean because they can be trained to use a **litter box**!

BRUSH

What Do Bunnies Eat?

Bunnies only eat plants. They need fresh hay to eat all day to keep their teeth healthy. Vegetables are the perfect dinner for bunnies. Fruit can help you train your bunny, but they should only eat it in small amounts.

HAY
CARROT

Funny Bunny

Bunnies can learn tricks like spinning, jumping, and even kicking a ball! Use fruit and a happy, quiet voice when practicing. Bunnies will want to play the most in the morning and evening. What will you teach your new bunny?

Keeping Safe

Bunnies get scared easily and may bite you when they're scared. To pet a bunny, sit quietly on the ground and let it come to you. If it feels safe, it may sit near you while you read, draw, or do homework!

It's important to pet bunnies **gently**. And when they hop away, that means they don't want to be petted anymore. Only adults should pick bunnies up because they get hurt easily. Put them in a quiet room when people come over so they don't get scared.

Name That Bunny!

What will you name your bunny? Some **popular** names are Thumper, Bunbun, Fluffy, Peter Cottontail, Honey Bunny, Bugs, Flopsy Mopsy, and even Jellybean! You could name it after its favorite vegetable, your favorite book character, or just something silly!

KINDS OF BUNNIES

LOP-EARED REX

CASTOR REX

FRENCH LOP

DUTCH

GLOSSARY

affectionate: acting in a loving way

comfortable: feeling safe, happy, and calm

gently: in a quiet, soft way

groom: to clean

hutch: a pen or cage for an animal

litter box: a box that a pet can be trained to go to the bathroom in

popular: liked by many people

FOR MORE INFORMATION

BOOKS

Gardeski, Christina Mia. *Pet Rabbits: Questions and Answers.* North Mankato, MN: Capstone Press, 2017.

Heneghan, Judith. *Love Your Rabbit.* New York, NY: Windmill Books, 2013.

Sexton, Colleen. *Caring for Your Rabbit.* Minneapolis, MN: Bellwether Media, 2011.

WEBSITES

Carrot Quest Online Game
hellokids.com/c_31060/free-online-games/online-games/carrot-quest
Be a bunny and find those carrots!

Fun Bunny Rabbit Facts for Kids
kidsplayandcreate.com/fun-bunnyrabbit-facts-for-kids/
Learn about rabbits in nature and so much more!

The Bunny Jokes Page!
members.iinet.net.au/~rabbit/rabjokes.htm
Tell these funny bunny jokes, or write your own!

INDEX